Irony and Irreverence

Irony and Irreverence

Michelle Hartman

ISBN: 978-1-942956-02-0
Library of Congress Control Number: 2015935099

Manufactured in the United States

Lamar University Press
Beaumont, Texas

Acknowledgements

Poems, some in altered forms, first appeared in these books, journals, collections and anthologies. The author thanks the editors of these publications:

Agave Magazine
Apparatus Magazine
Blue Hole
CALYX
Carve
The Centrifugal Eye
Concho River Review
Crannog (Ireland)
Dead Mule School of Southern Literature
descant
Disenchanted and Disgruntled
Illya's Honey
Melancholy Hyperbole
Poetry Pacific
Pushing the Envelope: Epistolary Poems
The Raleigh Review
Red River Review
San Pedro River Review
Texas Poetry Calendar
The Weight of Addition, an anthology of Texas Poetry

My thanks also go to the Dallas Poets Community for workshop help and to Ann Howells, Alan Gann, and Travis Blair for reading and critiquing. I am especially grateful to Bob McCranie for his editorial tutoring and the opportunities he has given me.

Poetry from Lamar University Press

Alan Berecka, *With Our Baggage*
David Bowles, *Flower, Song, Dance: Aztec and Mayan Poetry* (a new
        translation)
Jerry Bradley, *Crownfeathers and Effigies*
Chip Dameron, *Waiting for an Etcher*
William Virgil Davis, *The Bones Poems*
Jeffrey DeLotto, *Voices Writ in Sand*
Mimi Ferebee, *Wildfires and Atmospheric Memories*
Ken Hada, *Margaritas and Redfish*
Michelle Hartman, *Disenchanted and Disgruntled*
Katherine Hoerth, *Goddess Wears Cowboy Boots*
Lynn Hoggard, *Motherland*
Gretchen Johnson, *A Trip Through Downer, Minnesota*
Janet McCann, *The Crone at the Casino*
Erin Murphy, *Ancilla*
Dave Oliphant, *The Pilgrimage, Selected Poems: 1962-2012*
Carol Coffee Reposa, *Underground Musicians*
Jan Seale, *The Parkinson Poems*
Carol Smallwood, *Water, Earth, Air, Fire, and Picket Fences*

For information on these and other Lamar University Press books go to
www.LamarUniversityPress.Org

For more information about Michelle Hartman's writing got to
http://www.pw.org/content/michelle_hartman

This book is dedicated with gratitude and appreciation to:
William N. Drake, M.D.
&
Eugene R. Posnock, M.D.
&
their Office Angels
for keeping me alive and breathing so I can write

Legal Disclaimer

All characters and events in this publication, other than those clearly in
the public domain are fictitious and any resemblance to actual persons,
living or dead is purely coincidental.

    Except for you Eddie, I meant every word
I wrote about you. And as for my inbreed
happy-clappie in-laws, most of whom are outlaws
I don't have to worry because
the majority of you cannot read.
I did not leave out those marvelous blind dates
    sweaty, butt-crack guy
      and peely, unibrow dude
who promised to bomb my womb with their big cannons.
So while I'm clearing the poetic air
Fred, there is no such thing as necrolepsy and
Salmonella Faye, stop telling people that your name
is French, your family is white trash. I've lived among
the gilded vice of forgive-all, prosperity gospel, haggard harpies
(yes, we staked her, but I'm making no promises)
and suicides adjacent. Really, the rate on my paternal side
is ridiculous.
But all the rest of this conforms absolutely
with what the money-grubbing blood-sucking,
lawyers told me to write.

CONTENTS

Crazy Family

Addicted to Writing

Poetic Love

a poetic lover

         she said with gravitas.
And I am stymied, my mind off and running
through excremental laden minefields.
Is how do I love thee, foreplay?
Does he quote Keats and Wordsworth in bed
or maybe Byron and Marvell would be more
appropriate; or John Donne, the one
about stiff compasses?
Maybe he moved in poetic rhythms
AB AB AB ABBA ABBA ACDC AAAAAAAAA
or straight iambic pentameter with a flourish
of Shakespearian Sonnet to close.
Did he use strawberry enjambment
as love gel or have a recording
of Robert Hass's reading
at the Library of Congress playing
softly in the background?
Are the sheets peony blue scented
with sunshine's blush or does he reek
of woods and musk? Then she wanders
into post cocktail crowd, and I'm left wondering
if a rough rogering from a rogue construction worker
wouldn't do her a Bukowski world of good.

a proper love poem

He told her how big his library
was; of course men always
brag regarding size. But his living room—
to say it was book lined
is less than generous, completely inaccurate;
it was book crammed, book piled, book besotted.
A book store aroma with wall to wall shelves and tomes
on the floor, on windowsill and chairs
on every flat surface and even, defying gravity,
balanced on curved and angled ones.
He lit a fire, brought out cheese, bread and wine
while he talked of stalking literary characters
and the emotional damage caused by
mid-twentieth century British plots.
He asked for second date, dinner and a book sale.
She is thinking of boy names, Heathcliff or Roderick.

Grandmother got game

             joined a gym
lost flour-sack dress
a bit of dermabrasion here
laser there—
here a nip, there a suck
everywhere a tuck tuck
she liked it new, liked it crazy
new clothes, designer fragrance
the cottage sported deeper colors
washable fabrics
she liked it natural, liked it real

prowled pubs—seen leaving
with woodsmen, hunters—
he wasn't wearing a false front
did nothing to hide toothy grin
she liked it burly, liked it raw
she liked it when the wolf ate her

dead man's hand

she didn't mind the house work
        busy hands and all that
after all the wee ones had saved her life

her feet hung off the bed
        the little shirts did not fit the ironing board
still she smiled
        and blue birds were drawn to her shoulders
she meant to be grateful but one little hand
        kept venturing under sunny yellow skirt
        slid inside bright blue blouse
smeared porcelain skin with coal dust and worse
        left grime marks on her only dress
she prayed and struggled for a thankful heart
turned the other cheek— only to have it pinched
she never intended to strike
        but it was baking day
        and the rolling pin was in her hand
just a thud, such a slight sound and the eighth,
        and most annoying dwarf
        Gropey
        was forever gone

theoretical lying

This begs the question. She asked,
does your wife know about us?
Because once upon a time
in my salad days
I awoke next to an especially fine
young man while staring down the barrel
of a politically incorrect accessory
(read gun)
I do not want that to happen again.
Not that you are not fine and worth the effort
but age has made running
and dodging more difficult.

Of course, he replied, I no longer have enough
foot speed for adultery and other blood sports
or time for added laundry.
Let's just keep it theoretical....

The Character of Mistresses
after Ann Howells

Mistresses are not clock watchers;
seeing you, best part of their lives
they take time, demand
it in fact. A rushed hand gives
reason to leave. If you marry
they will toughen and dry
become bitter with suspicion.
But allowed to linger, baste
in sweet condos, lavish
immersion in trinkets, baubles
they bubble sweet, pungent.
San Trope bathers in July sun
they wallow
they luxuriate, voluptuous, firm
then lie back and dream of marriage.
Life is good.

A mistress never asks
if you're done? And a wife
never asks you to begin.

what came first, the chicken
(a poem in two voices)

    or the egg?
In Judeo-Christian-Muslim ethic
it would be the chicken, as God
                      (I believe the waitress was first, then
                             his secretary)
created the animals in the garden;
life was good. They received names
there was nice weather, then man
                     (friends tell me it's not important; but for me it's
                         vital to know exactly what happened, when)
fell and death came to earth.
Animals dying off needed replenishment
so procreation was added to the mix

thus the egg followed the chicken.
                     (logic in this situation is a chocolate frying pan
                         or Zimbabwean government stock)
In the creationist point of view
there was a single cell which split
into groups forming amoebas
then bigger and different animals.
                     (I'm not so stupid if it was pure love in the
                       beginning and then went wrong.)
Given that an egg is a single cell
fertilized by another organism
it would seem the egg was first.
                     (But if he was banging a bridesmaid in the
                     cloakroom then he needed to die)
A good Buddhist will tell you neither
exists, as they are visual perceptions
or manifestations of unschooled thought.
                     (The funeral was a love him and shove him
                     affaire)

The chicken that I see
and the egg that I taste
are not the same for you.

(Now I've got all the time in the world to decide
what comes next)

the best way to a man's heart
after Laurell Hamilton

       is six inches of tempered steel
briskly applied between his ribs.
Oh, four or five inches might
get the job done
but to be exact
you need six.
Ironic how phallic objects
are more desirable
the longer they are.
Anyone, who says size
doesn't matter
has been using
knives that are far too short.

still life with joy

The poet contemplates
waits patiently for inspiration
but she does not see the vase.

The lone iris   black   brittle
weeks old stem
folded over   pointing polar south.
The bud vase diameter
only one stem width
a designer sketch woman's curves;
pure crystal catching sun's rays
throwing blue   red stars
on opposing walls.
She has no pity for dead flowers
seeing naked bodies
writhing on grandmother's
walnut dining table
legs and arms create
living floral arrangement:
so a lovely penile stem
as focal flower, backed
by two small plums as filler.
Still lifes are so restful.

It Could Have Been Lubbock
after Alan Gann

It could have been Lubbock
and we could have been working at the feed lot.
But it was Batesville, Mississippi and the breeze
blew the odor of fried onions from the grill next door
tears from the smell and you brushed them back
while the guy next to us sang.

...nobody knows the trouble I've seen
...nobody knows my share of sorrow
We sat silent hoping no one would notice us
'til the biker guy started circling and you took my hand.
We cheek walked 'round that cell.

Dodged, as a hopeful con slid his hands down your arms
waltzed that our backs might stay against the wall.
As you begged the guard to allow one more phone call
he kissed your forehead with the sweetest, sweetest
no.

So I bailed out and you made love
in a tiny cell on the left bunk, after you smoked a cigarette
with someone named Earl
while Willie sang "Whiskey River Take My Mind"
on the guard's radio.

it's not delusional

A white washed room, eau de sausage and wood rot
mismatched chair circle and women various ages, sizes

they smell of White Diamonds, despair and Campho-phenique.
Stalker, obsessed, fixated has been used

to describe each of them at some point. Therapy
has failed, society crucifies them

they sit, shoulders drooping, eyes transfixed
on boxes in their laps, heaped to overflow

mementos, some honestly acquired, most stolen
from Tom Selleck or hunk of the day. The most envied

hold official envelops, restraining orders as badges.
Today is the day we burn our treasures, start

a new path, face dragons and other useless clichés.
Absent fathers, abusive mothers, husbands, reason

not a good excuse. In moments we will march
outside, cleanse ourselves with fire. I will not cry

as flames lick and tickle plush fake mustache. For
I know who, duct-tape bound, waits in my cellar.

Political Frolic

Five Little Lawyers Jumping on the Bed
For Dorothy Alexander

Five little lawyers jumping on the bed
    one fell off and bumped his head.

He sued the furniture manufacturers
the paramedics
and the hospital.

Four little lawyers jumping on the bed
    one fell off and bumped his head.

He formed a PAC to lobby furniture
laws regarding no corners and padded edges.

Three little lawyers jumping on the bed
    one fell off and bumped his head.

This lawyer rallied Conservative Groups
and had bed jumping declared an Official Act of Satan.

Two little lawyers jumping on the bed
    one fell off and bumped his head.

Receiving a level three concussion
and lingering brain damage
which caused him to read Dr. Seuss
in inappropriate places, at inappropriate times.

And the last little lawyer, she snuggled
down into that big empty bed and
dreamed all night
of shoving greedy bastards off the bed.

Cold Hard Truth

A great mound of raw dirt rose
next to the highway
beside it an echoing hole.
Progress marching ever onward,
society's ravishing need for yet another
home improvement store or pharmacy.
December's icy winds swirled around a
Port-o-Let huddled atop the mound.
A common man's statement,
easily seen from the busy road.
We have the same needs as you,
in your expensive vehicle.
Snow, usually unheard of in Texas,
the thickness of a baby's blanket
lies soft around the receptacle.
The sky blue of the box
seemingly from the chill
rather than manufacture's design,
speaks of the vulnerability
of those low paid workers,
off only due to the high holy days.
So much this quiet scene wishes to say of
desperate dreams and broken ambitions,
yet all I can think as we wait
patiently for the light is,
Boy, I bet that seat is cold.

Did I ask for your rib?

If God created Adam
then changed the design by removing a rib
if we discount Darwinism and its proof
DNA—then all men should have one less rib than women.

No one asked for a rib.

There was a book, male composed, product of patriarchal society
 justification of suppression, one of the best-known contributors
 to maintaining the inferior status of women.

I do not recall asking for a rib.

I do not decide what is legitimate rape, what happens to my body
what I can take or remove, and in some countries
whether I can walk on the sidewalk.

God did not need a rib for Adam.

I cannot get the same pay, recognition and will always pay more for a
        car.

You cannot charge for a transplanted body part.

He said, I will lift you off this earth and transport you to place
where nymphs sing and angels dance; which turned out to be
a basement apartment at his mother's house.

Can I give the rib back now?

Sisyphus Redux

If you go around telling people
they are downtrodden, you tend
to make two separate enemies:
the people doing the oppressing
who have no intention of stopping
and the people who are being oppressed.
But people being who they are
don't want to know—they can get
quite nasty about it. And when they
ask for bread do not give them
crackers as the church does
and don't, like the state,
tell them to eat cake. Explain
that man cannot live by bread alone,
and give them stones. Teach them
to pray, give us this day our daily stone.
Point them towards a hill, then
they will have a lovely distracting goal.

Compounds Compounded

It's a small gene pool—
their founding fathers had sloped foreheads
to begin with. Decades of inbreeding
finally render the people,
perfect subjects for show and tell at Johns Hopkins.
Their tract homes are cut off
by moats of green, mosquito infested water.
Every domicile equipped with generators,
food and assault weapons are packed
warehouse style.
Logic here as productive as telling
Satan you backed over his Hellhound.
The only mercy a lock
on our side of the gate.

Little Bunny Foo Foo

          went stomping through the forest
his man breasts jiggling atop a distended belly
lettuce bio-engineering had not been his friend.
Scooping up field mice, slamming
them against trees, lowering competitive food group.
Along came a voter, and he said, *Little Bunny Foo Foo*
I don't want to see you messing with ecology.
If you continue I'll have you for my tea.

Little Bunny Foo Foo
          went stomping through the desert
demodicosis mange caused his skin
to appear reptilian; his legs elongated, muscled
from DDT and PCBs. He bitch slapped a Chupacabra
gave him a rough rogering regarding
his rabbit sucking ways.
Along came a voter, and he said, *Little Bunny Foo Foo*
I don't want to see you messing with ecology.
If you continue I'll have you for my tea.

Little Bunny Foo Foo
          went stomping through the prairies
radioactive rabbit pellets killing grass
poisoning buffalo and wolves.
Along came a voter, and he said, *Little Bunny Foo Foo*
I've been such a fool to let you ruin the world
now I'll have you for my tea. And he
turned Little Bunny Foo Foo into a teabag.

Bester Texas Opera Company

Misplaced grant monies brought
arts program to Bester Texas.
Mayor Chester Miller's daughter
former watermelon crawl queen
could hit high notes real good.
And, after all, they had those costumes
Red Cross sent for clothing
after the last tornado swept through.

The advanced students out to the high school
adapted Madame Butterfly. Now
it was Ms. Butterworth who hooked
up with the local Fish and Game agent.
He went off and married the daughter
of a Dallas used car dealer.
Upon his return, Butterworth
kills not only his kid but a couple of others
she'd had by various Huntsville inmates.

Music was a bit harder so the students replaced it
with quasi-appropriate rock ballads.
Man, it was so ELO.
Closing aria rained down on weeping townsfolk.
They all agreed Walter, from the gas station,
looked truly devastated by loss of his pretend son.
Walter allowed as he was simply
picturing gas prices going higher.
The next day bad news came in form
of Government auditor, not so much
to recoup the monies but to cover up the debacle.
Town council members grinned as they signed
confidentiality agreement.

They'd only spent a hundred fifty seven dollars
the three hundred thousand left bought
each of them a right fine bass boat.

Bad Move

In glaring white sunshine
Bill and Mary pick out
a new double wide
casket.
Flat screen TV imbedded
in lid, leather holstered
mobile phone nestled in satin
lining. Right to Die law opens
never imagined markets. Now
all can decide
if they are alive or dead
on any particular day
and seniors are moving
to simpler surroundings, convenience
and low-cost our new god.
Bill's son will call once a week,
see if they want to go to lunch
drop by with mail.

Today, I will reevaluate
my political leanings.

Hello?

> after Kate Griffith

Welcome to telephone banking
    to pay your charge card please press two
        to check your balance please check nine
to dance in fire until the end of your days
    please press three
Hi, this is Paul, sorry I missed your call, leave
    me a message at the tone, I'll get back
        to you when the shadows creep up over my lips
Which service do you require police, fire, ambulance or sorcerer
To cancel a debit please press star
        to send your soul across the infinite void
        faster than the blink of the mind dreaming in the moonlight
please press zed...   now

and we crash cars, walk off piers,
while twits tweet and thumbs fly
tiny buttons sending bits, bytes and round faces
to people who have given up life
want to die horribly under buses
tethered electronically to other frightened
insecure...

excuse me, I have to take this call

now I lay me down

two Flexaril, an Esgic, three Trazodones
and four Benedryls riding a cascade
of vodka should do the trick.

I pray the Lord

to keep me from poisoned air and water
CEO's stealing the future, Politicians who
degrade the unfortunate. Save me from
your followers, predators and husbands
who will beat me.

If I should die

from cancer caused by foods I eat
or materials in the walls of my home
if I should be killed by tornados, floods
or other acts of
                              You.

My soul to take

as I've already been taken
and death's embrace
holds no sting for me.

The Wolf got Trichinosis

Adult worms invaded muscle tissues
    before he went for treatment.
He sued the pig's estate citing disability
    unable to hunt, feed his family.

The pig's estates counter-sued for
    wrongful death and destruction of property.
Between Twitter, Internet and nightly news
    the argument spread.

There was Team Wolf and Team Pig
    with fights breaking out at Wal-Mart.
Televangelists condemned pig eating as deviant
    and prohibited by the Bible.
Democrats pointed out that a Head Start Program
    would have fed the Wolf.
Republicans countered with pigs should
    have been able to own guns.
Senator in the pigs district pork-barreled a grant
    to rebuild the houses as museums.
Monies raised on-line for Wolf's legal fees
    were seized as profits from the crime;
embezzled from the city account by manager
    who disappeared with his girlfriend.

Years later a small blurb in paper mentions
    Wolf found dead on skid-row.
The only ones living happily ever after were
    Attorneys for both sides who retired early
        from proceeds in off-shore accounts.

shallow observations

there's a woman in a nursing home
on the outskirts of town
believes when she dies Ernest Tubb
is gonna come and Waltz Her Across Texas
'cept Ernest ain't coming, 'cause he bought into the whole Heaven
          fantasy package
death is to be survived
and survivors are not attractive
rarely possessed with pert butts or high saucy breasts
tight little women standing next to me in the grocery store
don't bother
when the big one comes they'll be raped repeatedly
by marauding hordes
while the ugly will handle serviceable tasks
in a world where souls pay forty dollars
to stand in hundred degree heat at Six Flags, three screaming children
but resent standing in line at the DMV
sixteen dollars gets you a license to drive on Dallas freeways
where you'll promptly be killed
'cause Johnny can't speed
and the last sign you saw was Clean Dirt Wanted
Zen'll get you through the heat, this too shall pass
but brother, it'll pass faster with a work boot up its ass
providing said hole comes with more teeth than tattoos
unless you're in parts of this great land
where a man with all his teeth is the equivalent of a leprechaun
so if you find one   buy a lottery ticket it's your lucky day
but if all else fails play dead, it's working for the Indians
while the black man demands reparations and the old woman just
          smiles
asks him if whitey pays what he owes then what'll he give the Indians in
          back rent
that is if he takes time from celebrating a Christmas no one enjoys
and it's time to announce the holiday emperors' naked
so you kill his money dreams

discover the difference between a serial killer and an executioner is a
benefits package
'cept stealing if you don't already have money is a perilous thing,
means you're a democrat and if you're not my religion you're going to hell
course my address is already 4401 handbasket
and I'm just a crazy woman in a big gold dress but when I die

    when I die. . . .

Willie Nelson is gonna pick me up in Honeysuckle Rose

we'll smoke doobies the size of summer sausages
heading into the sunset
    we're gonna... ride... ride...ride.

A Little Perspective

Perspective

Of course
there is a hell
she said
and it has
an observation deck

so I may
stand and wave
to all those kind
souls below
who warned me
I would go there.

Perspective #2

I was husband number one's fifth wife.
In my defense I did not find this out
until after I was married to him.
I was wife number two
for husband number two
who incidentally, is now
married to wife number five.
Finally, I was wife number one
for husband number three.
I am not
hard to get along with.
I was jockeying for position.

Perspective #3

Pavlov's dog to Schrödinger's cat:
Watch,
when I do this
it makes him write on his pad.
But the cat does not hear because
he is pondering why none
of his litter mates are claustrophobic.

Perspective #4

pol·i·tics ˈpälə͜ˌtiks/
noun
I see a hearty back slap, you a carved hilt
sprouting between shoulder blade and spine.
I am privileged to see surprise, terror, grief
resignation and wonder,
an entire Bergman film in five seconds.
You witness a blossoming blood stain.
Now I think we both should run.

Perspective #5

it was Pandora's jar
      he said
it was a box
      she said

a jar
not until she opened it

good one
I win
only until I crack your skull
      with Pandora's jar

Perspective #6

Paintings on velvet aside
dogs cannot play poker
their faces pristine mirrors
of their souls. Joy, anguish
and puzzlement are as clearly visible
as fiery sky messages from God.
Now cats can have your house
car and first born,
and you will never see a tell.

Perspective #7

April, the cruelest month,
and a great many poets
are trying to write a poem a day.
The dirty thirty as it were.
My question: does a
well written suicide note count?

Perspective # 12
after Gwendolyn Brooks

We was cool. We
Now drool. We

Gum cheese. We
Loud wheeze. We

Sleep late. We
Just wait. We

Not immune. We
Die soon.

Perspective #14

Of course Republicans write
poetry.   But it has Seussical
rhyming, two prevalent topics:
money and God
with the meter skewed
to one percent.

Perspective # 15

Marriage is Amaretto sweet
until one night you overdo.
After that the slightest whiff
makes you want to vomit.
For the longest time you can't
think about it without nausea.
After a time you try a sip
and find you can keep it down.

Eventually,
you go back to drinking,
but you never forget
that first miserable night.

getting to know you
> after Dorothy Parker's "I wish I could drink like a lady"

As his lips whispered against my throat
I queried regarding his financial status.
As his tongue flicked my nipple
I inquired about his political leanings.
When he displayed considerable liberal assets
I asked, what's your hurry?

Perspective # 16

The poet jumped the
candlestick, over the moon
through hoops and higher
than any frog has ever reached.
His poem was rejected
as being too intense.

Perspective # 17

That was the year I stopped being
a woman. Botching routine hysterectomy
the doctor ignored my reports of pain until
an abdominal abscess sends me to my knees
in local bookstore. During hurried surgical
maneuver, they split me from stern
to glory hole, lifting and rinsing internal
parts and repacking them as Waterford crystal
stapling left over skin.
As I slipped into coma
dreaming last dream of unblemished
body entertaining Tom Selleck on beachfront.

Little knowing the bitter loss
would fuel my crone-like political poetry.

Ted Cruz vs. Chupacabra

Pumped and adrenalin fueled
after election landslide
Ted Cruz returns to his office.
Slides to a halt as door slams
noticing high back leather chair
corner of office, a Chupacabra
sits smoking Cuban cigar, drinking
Jose Cuervo in Waterford.
The Chupacabra speaks, accent minimal
"I eat what I kill."

Crazy Family

five-foot enigma
For Ann Howells

It's odd, my brother had two kids
by his second cousin, before
he married a stranger; my sister
had four kids by a stranger before
she married a second cousin
yet my sister's children
are the more seriously impaired.
Perched in passenger seat
she regales me with tales of family
as I drive from used bookstore to lunch.

Epistles from Dippy pour
out of a woman who writes Pulitzer poetry
give soirees worthy of Perl Mesta,
drinks three-dollar wine she buys at Texaco.

A five-foot enigma is my traveling companion
fiscal Republican but social Democrat
she refers to Christianity as
that whole Heaven fantasy thing,
helps build libraries in churches.

She kisses her dog on the mouth
knows what toast points are
and how many it takes to win a
trip to Maine. Her clothes are stylish
sunglasses smeared and crusty
there are wind chimes in her car.

Gathers people who are artistic
slightly damaged, as is the way of
sensitive souls, she mends them one by one.
Gentle suggestions, guiding nudges,

sheep are her favorite animal
she knows well how to herd them.

We spend the day in used bookstores
trolling North Texas area
searching for elusive first edition
that Larry McMurtry missed.
She likes her books with high body count
her coffee black, her men tall and stoic.
Gives me good advice, a rubber duckie
dressed like a hooker, shaking belly laughs,
serious doubts about her sanity.
She deserves to be a book but she's only
tall enough for a poem.

Lady Fingers

Mormons, Jehovah Witnesses, or vacuum cleaner salesmen
Mother considered anyone on the porch game.
A Great Depression childhood taught her
necessity of wasting nothing.
The fingers frozen until holidays, thawed quickly.
She would stand me on milk crate
covered in crisp, starched apron
after she removed nail
my small hands carefully plunged reamer
through skin casing.
Mother said my tiny hands were perfect for this job
however ripped skin would get my ears boxed but good!
Sliding them inside out and rinsing in sink
just like a varicose vein, we used wooden dowels
to keep them open while baking. Frying
made them crisper but was bad for Daddy's cholesterol.

After they cooled I got to stir the filling, Ricotta cheese
chocolate chips, licking my fingers
when Mother wasn't looking. Full decorating bag
was too heavy so Mother squeezed the filling
into golden skin tubing. Then she took
small amount of icing and corn starch mixture coloring it
50's lipstick red and brushed onto nail bed.
The very best part was adorning the other end
with costume rings from five and dime, a shake
of powered sugar and a drizzly line of chocolate syrup.
I've always wondered if holiday memories
are really of the food or the wonderful times
spent with family members in preparation.

An Irish Bar in Fort Worth

After one Guinness, my husband's
become Kevin Costner.
I'm channeling my Irish roots
raising money for a Celtic festival.

Two Guinness under my belt
I sing with the band,
request protest songs.

Add another Guinness,
and I can't feel my lips.
It's remembering I am
that me husband is Germanic.

A fourth golden goblet,
and I yearn to run off with Irish crooner
who's singing for free—
income potential of most
beleaguered emerald-eyed men.

Bartender brings two vessels of joy:
I want to free Ireland and Scotland
from stone-faced woman—
never the drinker her mum was.

Man next to me,
who now looks like Tom Selleck,
bribes me with hamburger,
all the trimmings.
Homeland will have to carry the yoke
a few more years.

But, one of these days,
I'll have enough Guinness in me
to fight the good fight,
and damn the English.

Springtime Buffet

Below my office window, in quad of grass
blanketed with blue bonnets
bisected by Hwy. 114 and MacArthur
are a dad and a couple of toddlers.
He has the tots propped amidst flowers and chiggers,
tripod and 20 megapixel camera at the ready,
Infinity SUV parked on
shoulder of access road
a bit too far away to make
a run for it.

As this scene plays out, I notice
from my 11th floor roost
that I am not the only voyeur.
Two buzzards perch on ledge next to window
and I can see the scene reflected in their eyes,
a tiny bit of drool on their beaks—
don't you just love springtime?

What is West Texas Like

       I was asked on recent trip abroad?
It appears there are too many Zane Grey novels
and too little truth about Texas
in faraway lands. Settling in, I proceed
to give a thorough tour.
First, you take a piece of paper and draw
a horizontal line across the middle.
Color the bottom various shades of brown
and for the top; use your azure crayon solidly.
Now hold the piece of paper at arm's length
turn in a circle and there is West Texas.
For a more accurate feel, on every tenth
turn fix a cotton ball somewhere
in the blue area; two turns after that
remove it.

But if being there is all important
    while you are turning
      have someone set your clothes on fire.

it's always in the basement

         the crazy aunt that cackles
head in a hatbox smiling as
a snake does before it bites you
deformed child moans for attention
squatting by over-stuffed boxes
of sorry about what happens later
hulking machinery and appliances
that whirl   thump   and squish
cobweb-shaggy corners
dark concealed spaces
tiny chittering glee made
by things that will eat you
maybe before you're dead
gargoyles, goblins and gremlins, oh my
Skelebunnies, Skoffin and Scholl
black creatures with glowing eyes
red eyes or eyes on floppy long stalks
hold mops covered in mold and intestines
portals to hell and deflowered prom
queens with tire tracks on their gowns
whispering walls lurk behind shelves
bearing dolls whose heads are half gone
spin around or disappear to reappear
when you turn away
your fifth grade teacher holds ruler
with honed steel edge which she smacks
on pipes, the chink chills your heart
smeared mirrors show people
long dead, clowns with blood stained chins
framed examples of dead relatives whose eyes
track you with hungry zest
smells of dust, dirt and wheezy things

and you cannot find, you will not find
the heart-shaped box mother sent you for.
It's in the attic—but that's a different nightmare.

Helpdesk

for Wesley Hartman

Know that as buds
burst through bare earth in spring ritual
it is a given that in six months time
a mower will be along to sever their heads
but they grow because that is what they do.
In much the same manner
the IT person answers the telephone.
He or she knows what's going to happen;
a confused frustrated keyboard jockey,
who's just watched the entire July figures
"plionk' into cybernetic Armageddon,
desperate to find someone to blame.

In a way it's like the Salvation Army;
people tend only to call when
they are suicidal. The difference being
the Salvation Army is supposed to talk
them calmly out of that frame of mind
but the help line's function
is to channel helplessness and despair
into therapeutic rage aimed
at the poor fool answering the call.

Hello, this is Dave.
How would you like to kill me?

Gathering no Moss

Acid purple, neon green,
razor-headed youths
stare bewildered, Winnabegos,
old Cadillacs
fill music store parking lot,
walkers, canes, portable
oxygen tanks surround the
ticket outlet in two chains,
still growing

The Stones are coming to town.

Old hip flasks retrieved, filled
with Metamucil, stores sell-out
of hearing aid batteries,
physical therapy intensifies.

The Stones are coming to town.

Musings over the produce counter,
who will open for them?
Janis Joplin? No she's dead!
How about Dylan?
No, he had by-pass surgery last month.

They rush through the 4:30 sitting at
Denny's, cover themselves in Ben Gay,
pull out recently recovered Bic lighters,
wrap belly bags around San-A-Belt pants.
Between acts they'll rush the bathrooms
diuretic's on overtime, they'll free base
ibuprofen, old joints stove up from long
spells in small chairs.

Their children disapprove,
doctors shake their heads,

they'll be irregular for days
from greasy stadium food,
but it will all be worth it, because

The Stones are in town.

73

I'm fine, thank you

how are you is rhetorical
how was your meal
means leave a big tip

no one wants to hear
I'm slightly suicidal thank you
or *that oozing from my arm*
has subsided nicely

icy plastic faces greet
then woodenly
bid farewell
with *come again*

'till Tuesday
when the waitress asked
how I wanted my meat
and a dam burst
rising to my feet
I shouted

I want it cooked by a rugged craggy cowboy   who is naked from the
waist up slightly sweaty from the trail   a few scars telling of adventures
with a slight patch of hair in the middle of his chest he'll have heart of
gold and a grin that will open a nun's thighs   he needs me to take the
taste of the trail out of his mind   and I won't have a nice day until my
burger is done this way

they gave me pills
blue, red and green
electroshock
taught me
to make flowers
with tissues

I'm better now
but can't
go back to
Burger Barn ever again

a rose by any other name

A person's life is nothing more
than a series of tip-off's of what's to come.
I think if I'd had a hint, a map or a clue
it was being slapped with a moniker
like Jane.
There followed a childhood
no less bleak than that of Eyre
and nothing short of a calamity.
Teen years a plain girl, blindly following
any Tom, Dick or Tarzan
while supposedly funny guys with spotty faces
kept asking me what happened to Baby Jane?
Destiny had been sloppy with me
likely overworked by the rest of my woebegone family.
Kismet and Karma too flighty
to get involved and Doom couldn't be trusted.
Shaping up to have all the glamour
of a middle-aged, toll booth collector
I began using a lovely French, romance-laced
middle name of Michelle.
Michelle was a blank book
to be filled with fond fantasies;
which lasted until a fellow worker began
following me, singing, "Michel ma belle".
This led me to my second epiphany
regarding violence.

Addicted to Writing

flat pack poetry

Thin enough to slide under your door
yet able to transform into full-size villanelles
sonnets, ghazels and more.
Flat-pack poetry isn't just incredibly clever
this modern rethinking of verbiage assembly
is super-convenient, using slots and tabs
rather than dictionaries and thesauruses.
Best of all, flat-pack poetry is often
made from a single piece of imagery
and gets green points for ultra-compact shipping.
Imagine getting a pizza box dropped
off at your door and magically turning it
into a full-sized emotionally wrenching narrative.

Well, not a pizza box, exactly—more
an insanely clever pack of cardboard literature
fitting together into various configurations.
Each set contains five slotted idea modules
that can be connected with other sets
to create all manner of poetry, and other
forms of literature with bonus expansion packs,
novella, magnum opus and more.
Portability, sustainability and modularity give you
practical, simple and functional elegance
everything the world has always wanted in poetry.

So you've been accepted in Crannóg

I fell from step ladder, fall cleaning
bitten by spider washing out
air filter with hose, caught my hand
with trunk lid, but no worries
the bleeding seems to be ebbing.
Then you call to tell me
that you've been accepted into Crannóg.
Your poems, gossamer strands
of longing and desire usually preferred
over my radical, belligerent
long sloppy word kisses.
I grace blogs and occasional
narrowly themed issue of
No One's Heard of Us journal.
You are up for State Poet laureate
and I am reading to my granddaughter's
kindergarten class. And as I commiserate
with you over the impossibility
of your attending the reading in Galway,
I picture my well-chewed pen
embedded in your forehead;

right in the middle of my nom de plume.

W. S. Merwin has to die

There it is again, that bone chilling warning
at top of submission pages representative
authors are: W. S. Merwin, etc.

There is a perception filter installed on this
and every guideline page like it, whispering
to the subconscious; *move on, there is certainly*

nothing for you to see here.
If you turn on your magic subtext ring, it
reads, *don't even think about sullying*

our mailbox with your puerile nattering.
It is not enough to use vague descriptions
of desired work such as thought provoking.

Porn is thought provoking!
Their specific requirements even more dastardly
involve fonts that were already archaic

when Gutenberg carved his first movable type;
fees requiring bank loans and response time
of "until Jesus comes back."

A friend wrote a poem about killing Billy Collins
for which he received a funny e-mail
from the Laureate himself.

I, however, will probably be hearing from Merwin's
attorneys. But until then I'll be working on what
to do about Edward Hirsch.

Some Assembly Required

If a man finishes a poem,
he shall bathe in the blank wake of his passion
and be kissed by white paper
                          Mark Strand

check mail each day
unadulterated glee greets
brown paper wrapped
splendor   my very own
build it yourself poetry kit
magazine advertised hours of fun
guaranteed poet laureate
in every box

I mix a pitcher
of Billy Collins
clear living room floor
shut dog in kitchen

tab A into slot B
makes the line passive voice
but a fold on line C causes
first verse to be different
tense than the third
second page of instructions
is in Japanese
disclaimer at the bottom
assures me that nine
out of ten poets
recommend the
Build a Poem Kit
tenth poet is dead

piled about me
mismatched adverbs stick
to dangling participles
secret cliché decoder breaks
as I pull it from its wrapping
on one side lay
several long lines
which bear no relation

to the subject

dog escapes from kitchen
swallows several adverbs
gerunds catch in his whiskers
waving as he chews
frustrated I shove
it all back into box
throw into closet with
unfinished zigsaw puzzles
half-done afghan
beaded Christmas ornaments
and turn on the TV

wearing a heart monitor and reading Alan Berecka

An over-worked nurse checks monitor leads
and promises sleeping pill right after
she does something evil to a poor soul
down the hall. Following several thrill-packed hours
in the ER, at one AM I'm
finally admitted. Next to the ice machine
across from medication room
I'm in the hospital equivalent of hot sheet motel.
I dig through hastily packed overnight bag
for literary saving grace. Soon I'm deep
in *The Comic Flaw*, titular irony not escaping me.
I am transported to New York where small boy
deals humor to a set of dysfunctional parents.
Confusing Polish anarchy and whimsy
result in bus trip, a Pilgrim's Progress
through Dantesque circles, and I start to laugh—
exhaustion and pain whipped with frustration
and a soupçon of morphine, heated until it bubbled
and roiled into hysteria soufflé with tasteful garnish
of tears. From somewhere distant alarms
nurses, orderlies laden with Spanish Inquisition
torture devices converge on my door.
Heart monitor wirelessly linked to computer array
safeguarded in asylum bowels
watched by tech jockey, texting his comic book order
has misread my overwrought glee as death throes.
An unappreciative sycophant places books
well out of reach, last nurse out watches me swallow
pretty colored pills and extinguishes the lights.
As I drift away the hall noises are replaced
with riotous calls of children's voices
baseball cards slapping and accordion polkas.

figures of speech

For some time I've used exaggerated body language
hip bumps, hand touches and euphemisms to get
my point across.
Stomped up to obvious line in the sand
with, *I bet you can...*
yet, nothing has happened.
Although figures of speech are indirect, they are designed
to clarify, not obscure. But you were absent that day
and I am growing older.
I say tonight we go to my house and take off our clothes.

You, lying on the bed will be Pearl Harbor and I
shall be a Japanese Zero.

In days to come when we are questioned about our limps
we can go back to speaking in metaphor.

there is a poem in that

Traveling to Oklahoma to read at Scissortail
I'm hopelessly circling a little town called Davis
because Google must hire meth heads to write directions.

There is a poem in that.

They've changed the names of the streets
who knew the hotel on Parkington
is now on Caesar Chavez.

There is a poem in that.

Reciting political poetry to college students
who think they can vote on Facebook

The people in the room above me
either bowled all night or were babysitting orangutans.

I couldn't drink at the cocktail party with laureates
because of medicine I was taking

Dropped spaghetti sauce down my shirt
right before reading but no one noticed
because they were transfixed by open jean's zipper
and trying not to laugh.

There is a poem in life's
slightly tilted facets
different light wrapped
in carefully chosen word wardrobe.

Poets Grocery List

1 gal milk
3 tomatoes
gerund stain remover
bag romantic lettuce
rat poison
yogurt
big pk. toilet paper
why doesn't he love me
frozen dinners
soup, potato and chicken metaphor with stars
oatmeal instant and sestina
pentameter butter
grape emjambment
6 pk. meter
mayo
fifteen years of my life
4pk. penultimate stanza
hairspray
couplet filters
paper towels
razor blades

on becoming the greatest poet in the room

My poetry techniques will never
be the stuff of legend; never
graduate to literary texts
or university lecture halls.
But I think with some focus
and possible passing of exorbitant
sums of money, I can become
a strong presence in chat rooms.

a stranger in a strange land
For Paul Sampson

       wants to publish my poem if
I allow him to remove the parenthesis, delete
second and fifth verses
change it to past perfect third person omnipotent

 omnipotent as only God will know
      what the new poem is about

poetic theology indicates when writers
go to Heaven, they meet only editors
     who are pathetically grateful for any copy

and when editors go to Heaven, all the writers
     are so desperate for approval
     they agree to any changes, however damning

since I have been both
     it's pretty clear I ain't headed for Heaven

so accept this long-winded way of saying, yes
     you may remove the parenthesis, change
     this lament regarding childhood sexual molestation
     to coming of age angst
And thank you for accepting the rest of the poem
the handful of punctuation makes a nice fractal design

Selling Poetry to a Lout at the Local Bookstore

Eagerly I wait in Customer Service booth
serve those hungry to learn.
Man approaches talking into cell phone
Brow beating underling in his office
pauses long enough to throw request my way.

I need something by that poet,
I think they killed themselves.

Aha, Sylvia Plath?
No
Richard Brautigan?
No

He speaks into the phone,
I've got this little gal trying
to find a book for my Tiffany.
Tiffanys, I want to tell him, don't read poetry.

He returns to me, *I think it was a "Messkin."*

Pablo Neruda, Sandra Cisneros?
Although they didn't commit suicide.
No, he says frustrated.
Hears something in the phone.
Yeah, he was a homo.
How long do you have sir, I reply.

Look here he says into phone,
I got to go, these people don't know nothing.

He dials home, asks about poet,
Jack Keroac he says, got any of him?

Fresh out, I say, sold last one this morning.
But Waldon's at the mall has a whole section.

I cannot help you with this poem

I have never read Simic or Neruda
        Williams or Dickenson.
Poetry makes me itch and wheeze
so I write
but never read it.
I don't know which poem of Simic's
this is about nor do I
understand the word *ephemera.*
When I looked it up
it was defined by words I didn't understand either:
"Ephemera is plural of ephemeron; an ephemerid."
Another dictionary said it was something
designed to be short-lived or ephemeral.
But this poem drags on for days
so that can't be right.

It probably means your poem will be a big hit
among academic poets. But while I can't fathom
the poem's meaning, I like its imagery.

Except, is the "it" referred to in *when it says lavender
fields read rumpled counterpane*
the dog mentioned in the beginning?
(And I had to look up what counterpane means).
But I loved, *each time it says ocean think American in Paris...*
does that "it" refer to an ephemera?

Though I am lost in the meaning of this poem
I'm having my first cup of coffee now
I'm sure it will be clear as hell in just a little while.

how to catch a poem

between rosemary and dark purple pansies
it huddled shivering
behind yard gnome
dressed as Christmas Elf

armed with water can I go
back and forth   kitchen sink
to various pots leaving
front door ajar   humming
seasonal tune
I track it peripherally— as growing bolder
it sidles into warm house flitting
from couch to bookcase
a Super Secret Squirrel

knot of excitement grows—
my gut gripped by long writers block spell
I want to sweep it up—look for meaning and insight
but calm prevails
as during afternoon
I catch sight of scarlet billows
royal blue portals   winged horse
      cascading harlequin clowns

as dusk drapes mauves and grays upon windows
the poem perches upon desk top
acquiescent smile
      and lovely line breaks

Dear Poet
> for Dr. Jeffery DeLotto

I have at last scored
a copy of your first book;
found Saturday
huddled in second hand bookstore
an inscription reads
for a fellow writer and a fine student.
No name however
so I assume the universe intended it for me.
It is well read
but still in tact. (I meant that spacing).
And it quickly curled up alongside
a British mystery and Terry Pratchett satire.
Several minutes later
I had to speak tersely
when I caught it trying
to toss a Billy Collins hardback
out of the cart.
But it now snuggles happily
on the shelf down in the Z's.
Just in case.

a sudden discovery of hands
Scissortail Literary Festival 2014

Big poetry festival
and in the midst
of first poem I discover
my hands are flapping in the wind;
like those red motorized blow-up figures
wildly gesturing outside new gas stations
or shoe stores
and this crowd terrifies me.
I tuck them in back pockets but this evokes county hick look.
Hands in front pocket jingle car keys
but they must not be allowed flight again.
A brilliant idea; grab the lectern!
And I do, knuckles white, damp upper lip
I lean in as though resisting gale force winds.
Only to discover my breasts
cover the bottom of poem I am reading
and I think the people in front row look afraid
of this maniacal poetry rendering
in Mississippi preacher on-fire manner,
poet who appears ready to fly right over that lectern.
At moment of despair I reach end of final poem
taking my seat
and rascally hands flop into lap
exhausted by extemporaneous performance,
lyrical exuberance.

Nursery Rhyme Prediction

> There was a man and he had naught,
> And robbers came to rob him
> —Mother Goose Nursery Rhymes

All great stories possess a violent element.
Ponder if you will
something lurking at your door
huff and puff
lacking sympathy or forethought
to callously blow your house down.
Dehumanizing as the nightly news.
But where would the Three Little Pigs be—
three differently-gendered individuals
living a life that defies societal norms?
And no one would have heard of them
unless targeted by religious groups
who felt pig eating defied Biblical strictures.
Stories of peace and placidity
are not reported by bleached blonds
with enough grease paint to lubricate a Hum-V.
Violence, officially denied
is necessary for change
is indoctrinated into our children.
The perilous story
of middle class economics
without a peep or a whimper
they all fall down.

Halleluiah Sacramental Poetry Militia

fresh April day they gathered, poets
young and old, sober and crazy
to read and rejoice in the spoken
word, the bond of verbal
struggle and the free eats

can I get a halleluiah

used book store with poems
pinned to the wall, post office wanted
have you seen this poet?
Brother Alan his bare feet
cleansed in the steam of symbolism
kludged together a sound system
as Sister Melanie led
us off rapping the opening
lines to the Canterbury tales, middle English
never sounded so spiritual

and they came throughout the day from far
away as Tucson bringing the word, keeping
the faith, Sister Ann got out her tambourine
but the donations flowed in because Ann
can't play the tambourine and no one wanted
to have to wrestle it away from her

can I get an amen

and they testified, Brother Travis told
us of the wages of sin and taking Quaaludes
with Willie and Brother Bob told us of a child of God
beat to death because of ignorance
and hate and the crowd was swaying
to the rhythm of fiery thoughts

visions of lovers locked in the throes of doubt
regret and booze

can I get an amen

the sick were brought in their pockets full of verses
while sweet Sylvia fed the masses with strawberry enjambment
and Brother Clebo told us of love supreme
          supreme, supreme

we rode rockets and dreams out across the plains
and back, to people dancing while they read poetry
screaming about the kangaroo on the corner
of walk and don't walk and we hugged and cried
pressing pamphlets and bits of paper in each other's hands
as though they'd keep cancer and the devil away
while every different god was mentioned
and the words flew

flew right up into the sky
right up into heavens

like tiny white doves up into the heavens
our offering to the universe

amen

Written in celebration of the 20th Anniversary of the Dallas Poets Community- 14 hour poetry
reading, April 10th 2010.

Book Club Discussion Questions

1. Between your work, family and spa time let's assume no one read past the first ten poems. Discuss where you think this book will lead if you are ever imprisoned in a foreign country and this is all you have to read?

2. Has anyone ever read any W. S. Merwin, and, if so, do you think he should die?

3. Who picked this book? Why do you think Tiffany picked this book, since it's obvious she has never read anything but chick lit and usually doesn't finish that?

4. Does it come across that the writer prefers writing poetry or that her ADD makes longer works simply impossible?

5. Who brought this wine? I didn't know they still made Boones Farm.

6. Does this book evoke any emotions: rage, disgust or urge to sleep with dwarves?

7. Do you feel that the weak and useless men portrayed in the poems seem familiar? I mean really familiar?

8. Would you put this book on your coffee table or would you rather display a big name poet so people won't think you're shallow?

9. Can you see any of these poems being made into HBO specials, like maybe the one about Snow White killing the dwarf with a rolling pin?

10. What TV show were you actually watching while you were pretending to read this book?